God's Li'l People
and Miracles

True Stories About Little People
by Mama G.

I0169096

Illustrations by Young Artists:

Cover .... Shaylah Grech
Jordan .... Mark Dombowski
Li .... Megan Yoder
Michael............................. Hope Pigott
Debbie.............................. Jordie & Janae Dyck

Layout and Design...................... Diane Connis

Publisher……………................. Five Stones Publishing
International localization
network
Randy2905@gmail.com
www.ilncenter.com

ISBN: 978-1935018-88-9

Dedicated to our Dear Heavenly Papa who deeply loves ALL His little people everywhere

Introduction

This book gives a peek 'behind the scenes' when earth situations become 'impossible'. In that other realm we call heaven, there are no impossibilities.

God does something to fix the situation, and we call it a miracle.

What an adventure to gather and share these stories, for little people to know that miracles happen every day!

We are God's little people.
We got a light, and we're gonna let it shine!
We are God's little people.
God's little people are
God's BIG PEOPLE sometimes!

Bold print tells the story to little people, with added details for bigger little people.

Look for the dove in the pictures, a reminder of our loving Father's Spirit, who is always with us. Jesus said He would never, never leave us. ~ Mama G

Secrets For Big People

This is a day when little people are **BIG PEOPLE** in God's Kingdom. Little people live in spiritual awareness; they see monsters and angels. They have dreams and visits to Heaven. They hear **God** speak.

BIG PEOPLE teach them that Heaven and **God** are far away --that **God** doesn't speak much --that the Bible is hard to understand.

BIG PEOPLE often doubt; little people usually believe. Jesus said, "Let the little people come to me. Don't get in their way." (Mt. 19:14) He also said, "Until **BIG PEOPLE** become little people, they can't really see (into the real world)."

When little people arrive in this world, **BIG PEOPLE** think they don't know anything. **WRONG!** If you want to learn about the 'real world', find a rocking chair, and let a little person who is not 'brain-washed' with TV and fairy tales crawl up in your lap. Then if you really listen, you will learn.

A three-year-old was observed gazing at his new baby sister. Finally he leaned over and whispered, "Tell me about Heaven. I'm starting to forget."

God's Li'l People stories are shared in the simplicity of a little person's world, where anything **God** says or does is believable. It is my prayer that you will learn to know **God** better as you watch **Him** with the little people.

He gave us little people to lead us into heaven realm awareness. 'A little child shall lead them. . .' Half of people living today are under eighteen. But these 'heaven trail blazers' are one of earth's best-kept secrets.

Jordan

Would you like to meet Jordan, the Miracle Boy?

Jordan was five years old, and his family was moving
to the little town of Hickory in North Carolina.

**One day Jordan was playing outside in the yard. His
daddy was loading a BIG trailer in the driveway.**

It was a busy moving day. There was lots and lots of stuff in the yard.

All of a sudden, Daddy heard a BIG BUMP! and screams!

Oh, no!!! The trailer thing had fallen on Jordan's head!

It was a very heavy trailer ramp. With miracle strength his daddy lifted it off. Jordan was not moving, and his head was bleeding.

Daddy picked him up and ran to the car.
Mommy held Jordan, while Daddy drove
very fast to the hospital. They were
praying for their little boy to be OK.

When they reached the hospital, the doctors were very worried.
Jordan was still breathing, but his head was dented in.

The first hospital sent Jordan to a bigger
hospital in an ambulance with a siren.

Woo-woo-woo! Jordan was not moving.
His head was hurt very badly.

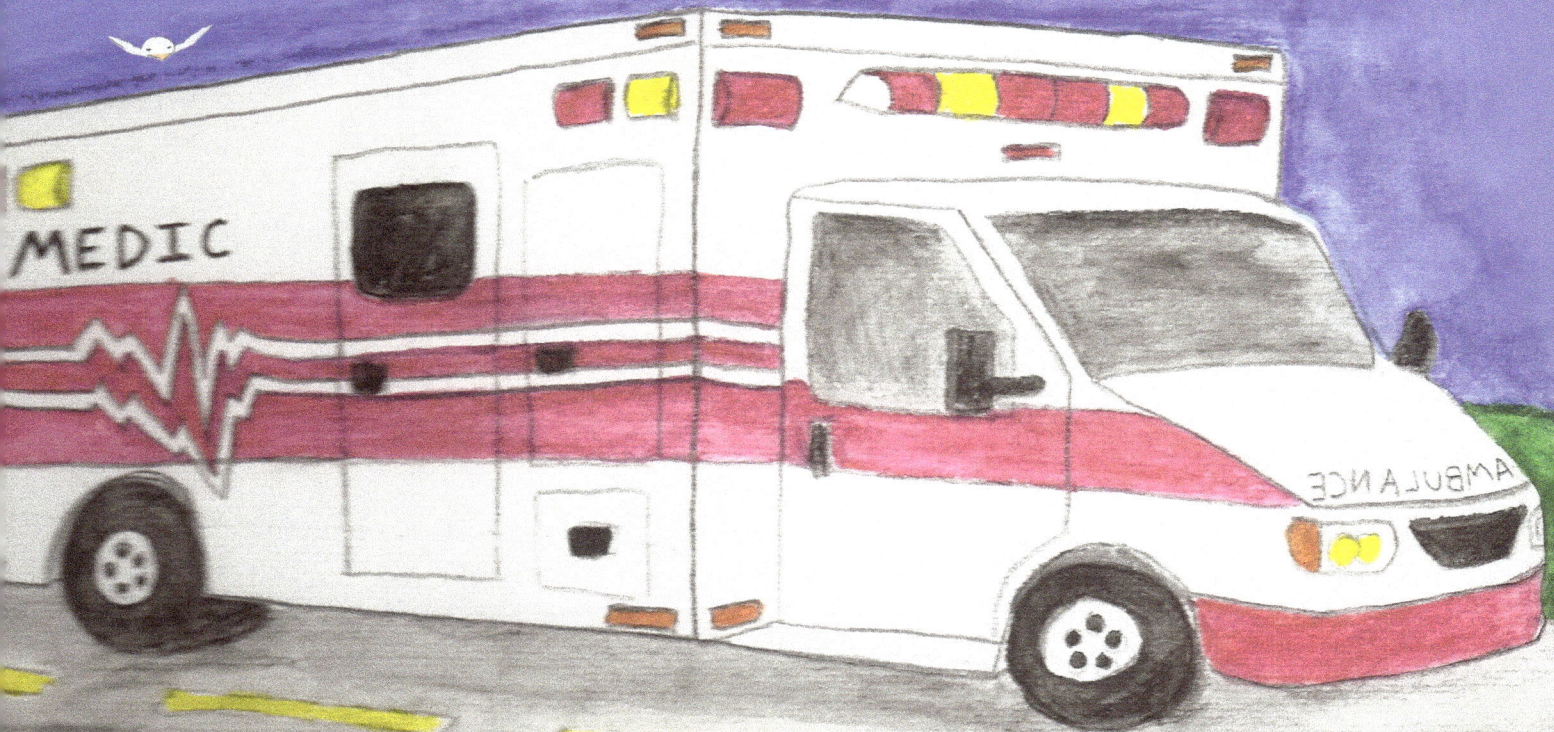

MEDIC

AMBULANCE

Suddenly Jordan sat up! It looked like someone lifted him up.

He opened his eyes and said, "Jesus! Take care of me!"
Then he closed his eyes and laid back down, fast asleep.

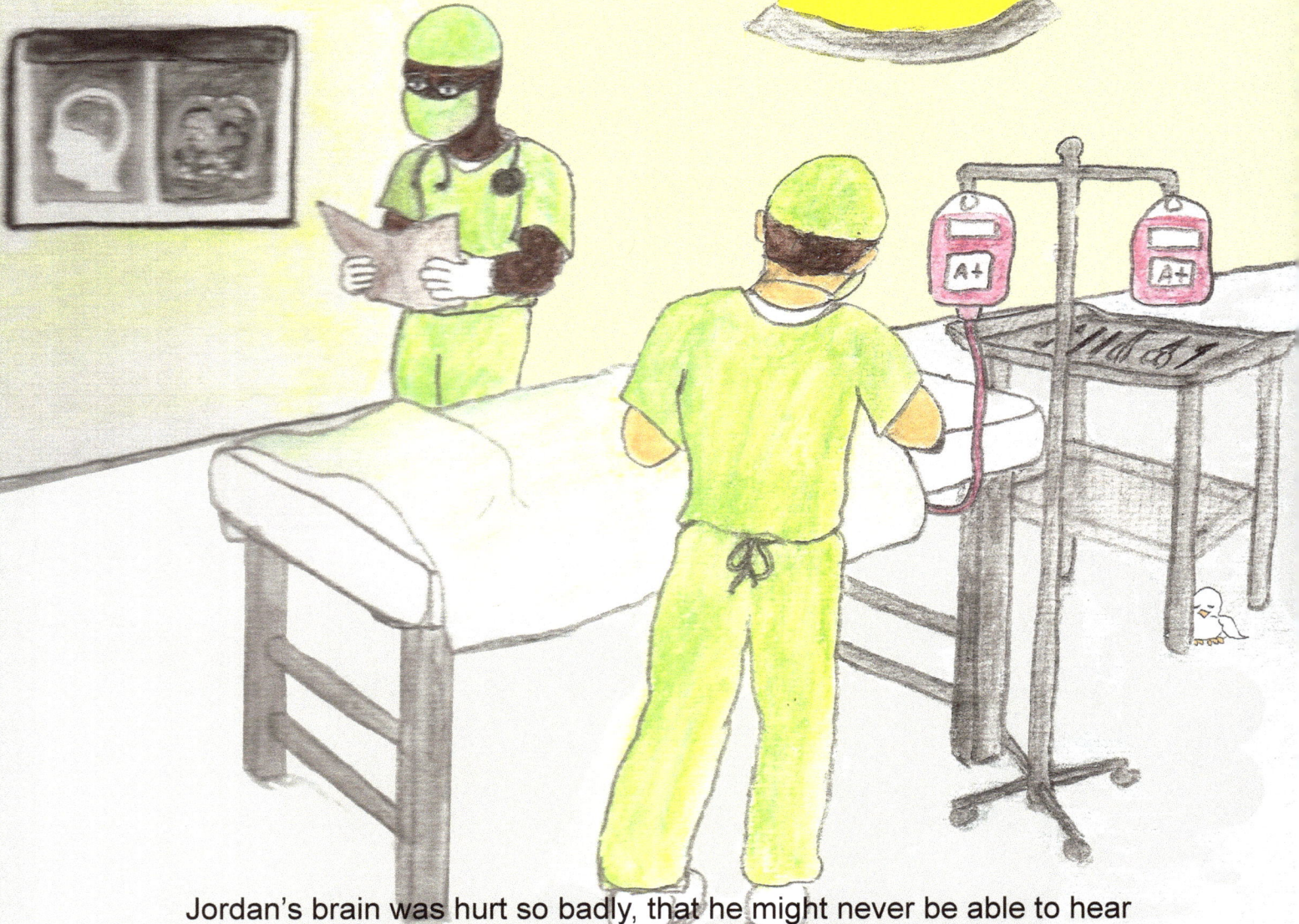

At the hospital, the doctor tried to fix his head.
He worked on him for many hours.

Jordan's brain was hurt so badly, that he might never be able to hear
or talk, or even think. The doctor did not know if he would even live.

Daddy and Mommy and their friends
held hands and prayed. They asked God
for a miracle for Jordan to be healed.

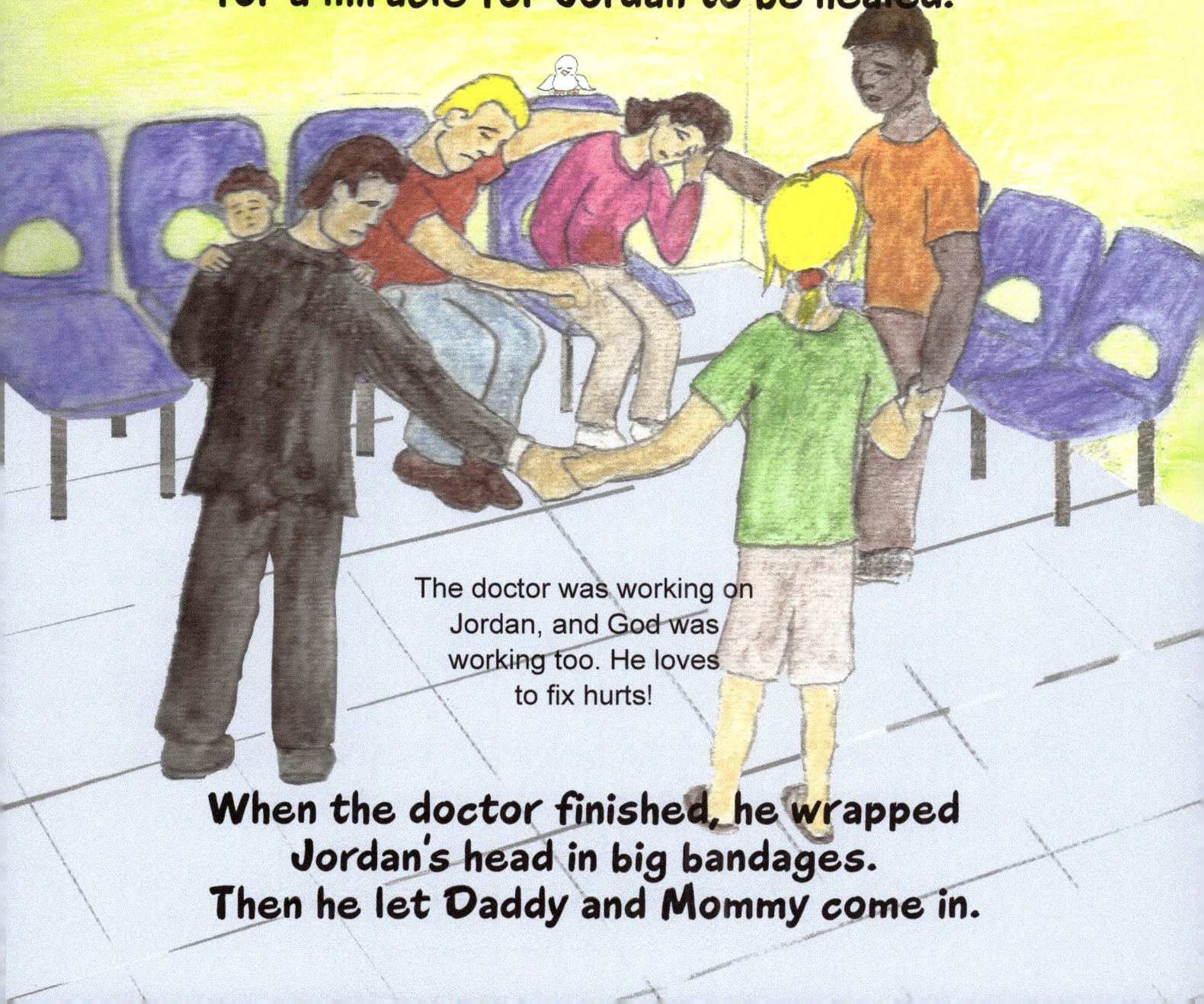

The doctor was working on
Jordan, and God was
working too. He loves
to fix hurts!

When the doctor finished, he wrapped
Jordan's head in big bandages.
Then he let Daddy and Mommy come in.

They tip-toed into the room, and Jordan opened his
eyes! He coughed, and said in a little voice,
"Excuse me."

He was alive!
He could think!
He could talk!
Can you guess how happy they were?

Mommy reached out to him with tears in her eyes.
She was so happy she was crying!
(Mommies do that sometimes.)
"Oh, Jordan! We love you so much!"

Mommy stayed beside him, all night, and all day.
The doctors and nurses called him MIRACLE BOY!
"How is he getting well so quickly? It's impossible!"

The doctor who first saw the X-rays of Jordan's head, came back to see him. He said, "I never thought your boy would be well, or even that he would live. I have never seen anything like this before!"

But Jordan knew. When he felt pain, he would always ask his Mommy to pray. And the pain would go away.

God healed him so quickly, the doctors let him go home after 10 days!

Very soon Daddy came to take Jordan home.

That was a happy day! Everybody was happy!

He said, "Mommy, you are my best nurse!"

He smiled as little brother hugged him.

For a long time, Jordan did not remember anything about the accident. But, one day when he was playing with his little truck, he suddenly remembered. "Mommy, I pulled the pin out—that made the ramp fall! It really hurt, but then Jesus came all dressed in white. Then Daddy came and lifted the ramp off of my head."

Jordan told his mommy and daddy that Jesus came to the hospital to see him. . . " Jesus lifted me up, and hugged me, and He said, 'Jordan, you're going to be O.K.'"

Then Mommy remembered when Jordan had sat up quickly and said, "Jesus, help me!"

So Jordan was a MIRACLE BOY!

It wasn't Daddy that lifted the heavy 300- pound ramp by himself. It was not only the doctor that fixed him. It was not the nurses that took away the pain, and made him talk and walk again. It was Jesus!

Jesus was there all the time-- loving, and holding, and healing Jordan.

Jesus likes to hug us, and make everything better. Sometimes He lets us see Him, and feel Him holding us. That is very special.

Li

Happy, little
Li lived in China.

She lived in Guangdong with her family. Li's daddy
worked very hard for his family to have enough rice to eat.

**Li and her family loved God. And they
told lots of other people about God's love.**

Then many people stopped worshipping idols, and started to love God, too.

One day bad people sent Li's daddy to prison, far, far away. They said, "You talk about God too much."

Li's mommy took her family to live near daddy. They traveled on the train for a whole week. And when they found the prison, they made a little hut nearby.

Daddy had to work very hard.
He could not go to the hut to see his children.

He worked in iron mines underground. It was very cold, and he didn't have much to eat. But he worked hard, and he told other men about Jesus.

God cries when people are hurting.
One day God let him go to Heaven to live with Him.
Then Li's daddy was not cold, or hurting anymore.

Heaven is a wonderful, happy place where Jesus and the angels live. There are no bad people there—only people who love Jesus and love each other.

Li cried when she heard her daddy was gone. Her mommy hugged her, and they cried together.

Now Daddy could never come to see them. What would they do without him? They were ver-r-r-y far from home.

Those were very sad days.

Li took care of her brothers and sisters while mommy went to work. But every day the baby cried for mommy.

One day, Li said, "Mommy, I will go to work; And you will stay home with the baby."

"Oh, my dear Li!" said her mommy. "You are not big enough to go to work." "Yes, Mommy," said Li. "I can do it. Jesus will help me."

Then Li walked down the road to the prison.

She told the director, "My daddy is gone, and we need food. I must have a job!"

And they gave her a job-- a very important job! She had to push a red button ONLY when the director told her.

She stood by the emergency button all day long. It was a loud siren to warn the men working deep underground to come out immediately.

Li was so happy to have money to buy food.

One day, when Li was at work, suddenly she heard a voice, "Press the button!"

She looked around, and did not see anyone. Again, she heard, "Quickly! Press the button!"

Then, again, she heard, "Li, you MUST press the button NOW!"

"It must be God's Voice," thought Li, so she pushed the button!

Li pushed the red button! The very loud siren sounded—Wo-o-o-o-o-o! The director was angry!.

Many, many daddies came running out of the ground. "Why did you push the button?" He yelled. "You made 3,000 men stop working and come out!"

All of a sudden, the ground shook! It was a big earthquake! And the whole mine fell down!

It totally caved in, and could never be fixed.

**Then it was very, very quiet.
Everyone was looking at little Li.**

The director quietly asked, "Why did you push the button?"

"Jesus told me to push the button," said little Li.

"I heard a voice. I looked around, but did not see anyone. Then I heard it again."

**" When I knew it was Jesus' voice, I had to push the button! He loves all of you very much.
He did not want you to be hurt."**

"Jesus is the only way to know God. You must love Him. You must turn away from your idols. He will forgive you and make you good—just like He is."

Then all the men knelt down and prayed.

Even the prison director said, "God, please forgive me!"
They were so thankful for a Daddy God that loved them and saved them
from being killed. They wanted to love Him always and forever.

Li's mommy said, "Li, I am so proud of you!"

Even though she was living in a little shack with no daddy or nice stuff, she was smiling. She had a warm, cozy feeling inside. . . because Daddy God was holding her tight, and she could picture her daddy smiling at her.

That night, Li went to sleep smiling, and dreamed sweet dreams. Good night!

Michael

"Why is everybody crying?" asked Michael. "Is something wrong with my baby?"

Michael was three, and he lived in Tennessee. He was very excited about getting a new baby sister!

"Yes," said Daddy, "She is very, very sick. They took her to a different hospital."

"When she was born, she could hardly breathe. Mommy is staying with her."

Michael and Daddy prayed. They went to the special bedroom Mommy had fixed up for the new baby.

One week went by. Baby was getting worse. All their friends were praying for baby, too.

Did God hear their prayers?

Did He love the baby as much as Michael did?

What a silly question!
God loved the baby so much more than we can even think!

God's love is so strong, He will do anything to help us—even if it hurts Him.

He is always watching, and waiting for us to ask Him to help us.

The doctors said, "There is very little hope. The baby is dying."

Michael was very sad.
He loved to sing to his little sister, when she was in Mommy's tummy.
Now he could not even be near her.

"Please let me see her!" begged Michael. "Please! Please! Please! I want to sing to her!"

But kids are never allowed to go in the hospital ICU. So what could he do?

God would have to make a way for Michael to see his baby sister. And that's just what He did. Mommy said, "You will see your sister, whether anybody likes it or not!"

And she dressed him in a big hospital gown, and marched him right past the nurses!

"Get that kid out of here! No kids are allowed in here!" shouted a nurse.

And Mommy said, "He is not leaving until he sings to his sister!"

Michael was already looking at his tiny baby, struggling to breathe.

He started to sing, "You are my sunshine, my only sunshine. You make me happy when skies are gray. . ."

Immediately the baby breathed easier. Her heart rate became steady.

"Keep singing, Michael," said Mommy.

"You never know, dear, how much I love you. Please don't take my sunshine away."

*"The other night, dear, as I lay sleeping,
I dreamed I held you in my arms. . . "*

The bossy nurse had tears in her eyes. And the baby relaxed even more.

*"You are my sunshine, my only sunshine.
Please don't take my sunshine away."*

Michael thought he saw baby smile as she went to sleep. The very next day, she was all better! and they got to take her home!

It was a miracle! Mommy and Daddy called it a miracle! The doctors called it a miracle! Women's Day magazine called it 'the miracle of a little song!'

Michael didn't know what a miracle was. But God knew, and together they were smiling very big smiles at the tiny baby.

Debbie

It was a snowy day. Five-year-old Debbie was in the backyard, sledding with her little sister and friends.

They were bundled up in snowsuits, mittens and boots. March is very cold in Pennsylvania.

"Mommy! Mommy! HELP! Come quick!" cried little sister. "Debbie fell in the pond!"

Mommy came running! She saw the sled, but she didn't see Debbie. "Oh, God! Show me where she is!"

Mommy tried to break through the ice, crying, "Dear God, where is she?"

Then Daddy came running, just as Mommy saw a little hand stick up through the broken ice! Daddy jumped in, and pulled her out. "Oh! Thank You, God! Thank You! Thank You!"

But Debbie was all puffed up, full of water. She was blue, and was not breathing.

Daddy started pushing water out of her tummy. He tried to help her breathe.

Daddy had just had classes to learn CPR. But he didn't know he would have to help his own little girl!

But Debbie would not breathe!
A friend called 911. Medics came.

But they could not make her breathe either.
They put her in the ambulance and raced to the hospital.

PARAMEDICS

Ambulance

Woo-Woo-Woo! When they were almost to the hospital, Debbie's heart started to beat, very faintly.

It had been 45 minutes. Mommy and Daddy were praying.
The medics were very surprised and said, "We could not make her breathe!"

They carried Debbie into the hospital.
But the hospital said, "We can't help her here."

So they put her on a helicopter to go to a better hospital.

"She probably won't live through the night," they said. "If she does, she won't ever think or talk or walk again. She will be like a baby all her life."

In the new hospital her heart kept beating all night. It kept beating for a whole week.

They stayed with her, but she didn't move and she didn't wake up. "Mommy and Daddy cried, and they prayed, "God, please make our little girl all better!"

Then after three long weeks, Debbie woke up! Her Mommy was so excited! "Oh, thank you, Jesus!"

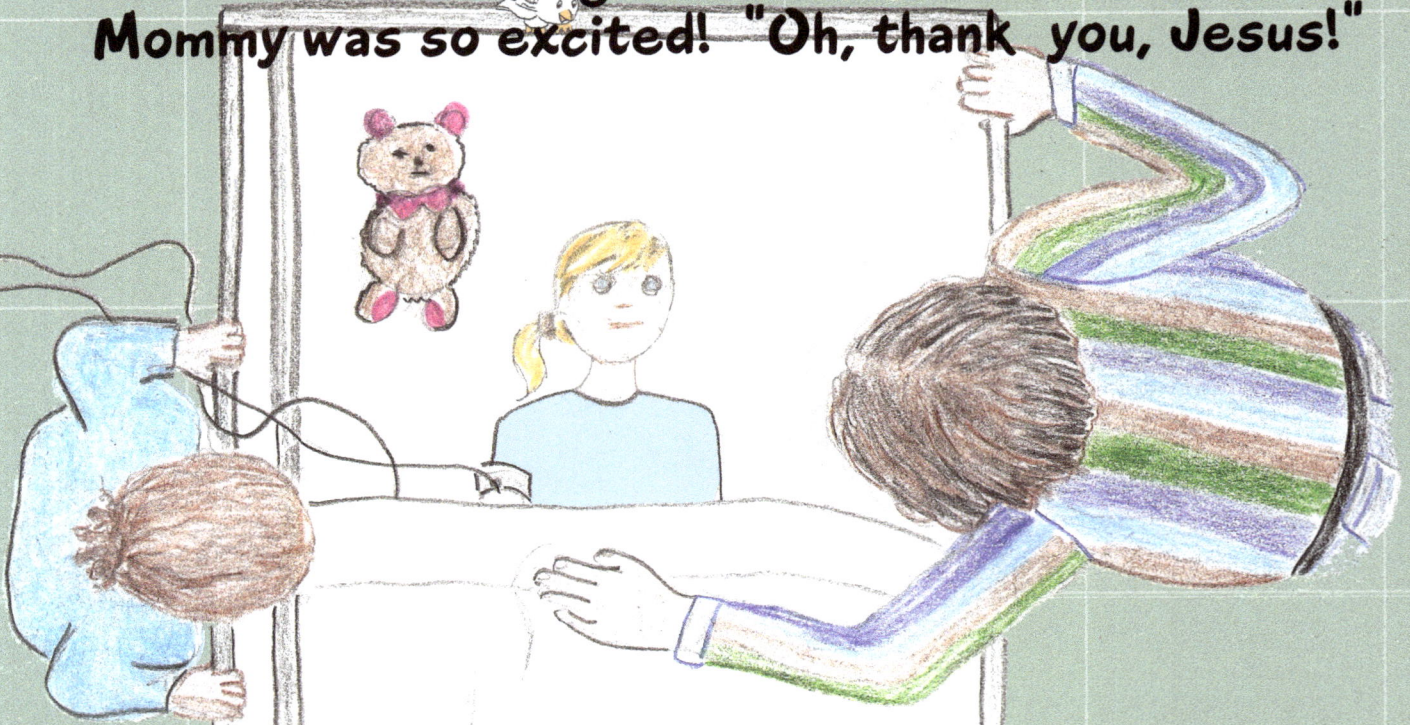

It was a miracle that Debbie was alive. It was another miracle that she woke up from her long, dark sleep, and that she could think and talk. Yet she could not see, and she could hardly move. Her long journey was just beginning.

That was a very happy day for Debbie's family. They laughed and cried, "Debbie is alive, and now she will get better!"

Debbie awoke on Resurrection Day--the day we celebrate Jesus coming back to life, three days after He died for us. It was the perfect day for Debbie to wake up.

Debbie did not remember what happened,
or why she was in the hospital.   But she was
very happy to have her Mommy close by.

She needed many more miracles, but she was alive! She had a family
who loved her. And, most of all, Jesus loved her and was always there with her.
He had good plans for her life, and He would heal her.

Many days went by. "When can I go home?" asked
Debbie. "Today!" said the nurse, with a smile.

So Debbie went home forty days after she had drowned.
She had to be cared for like a baby. Her muscles were flabby.
Her feet turned in. She didn't know how to walk, or even stand up.

From then on, mommy became the best nurse.
She took care of Debbie, and loved her, and
prayed for her.

One day there was a knock at the door.
A medic wanted to see the little girl who had died—
the miracle girl!

He said, "I was with her in the ambulance. But we were not able to keep her alive.
I heard that she came back to life! May I see her?"

It took a long time to get all better.
It was hard to make her arms and legs work,
but Debbie never gave up.

Mommy and Daddy never gave up.

And, of course, neither did God.

He did many miracles for her, until she could
walk and talk, and see, and do school work.

Jesus loved her very, very, VERY much.
He became Debbie's best Friend.

Every time the doctors said, "She will never . . . !"
God said, "She will!" And every time she did!

Watch For Our Other Titles Of God's Li'l People

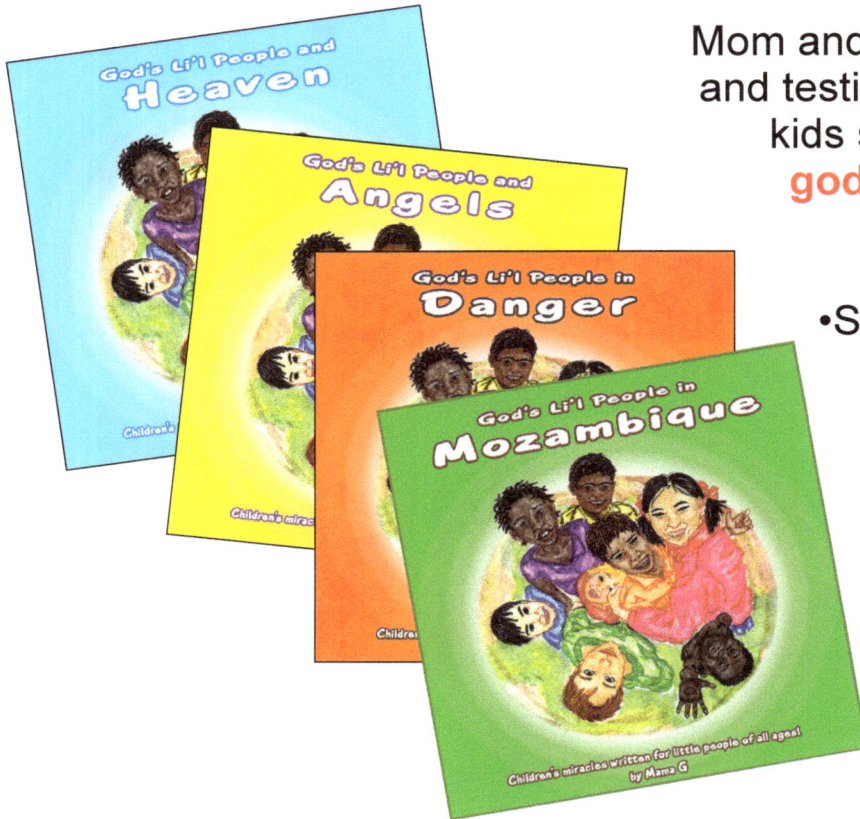

God's Li'l People and Heaven

God's Li'l People and Angels

God's Li'l People in Danger

God's Li'l People in Mozambique

Children's miracles written for little people of all ages!
by Mama G

Mom and Dad, find tools, links and testimonies about raising kids supernaturally at:
godslilpeople.com

•Share your experiences.

•Get updates.

•Order new books.

Find other language editions as they become available.

If you have a miracle story to share, or would like to do some pictures for a story, please write Thelma Goszleth at:

godslilpeople@gmail.com

www.ingramcontent.com/pod-product-compliance
Lightning Source LLC
Chambersburg PA
CBHW041436040426

42452CB00024B/2990